FOR YOUR HOME

FOYERS AND ENTRYWAYS

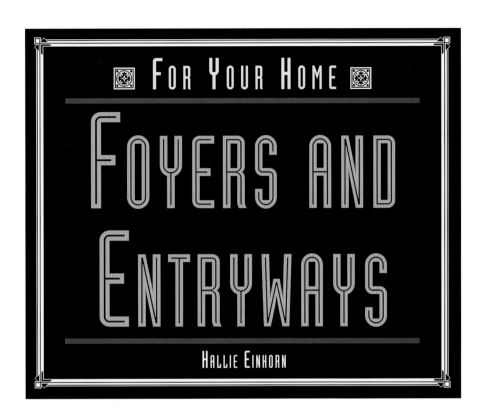

FOR YOUR HOME

FOYERS AND ENTRYWAYS

Hallie Einhorn

FRIEDMAN/FAIRFAX
PUBLISHERS

Dedication

To Linda and Joel Einhorn, for introducing me to the decorative world at an early age.

Acknowledgments

Many thanks to Sharyn Rosart for giving me the opportunity to write this book.

A FRIEDMAN/FAIRFAX BOOK

©1998 by Michael Friedman Publishing Group, Inc.

Library of Congress Cataloging-in-Publication Data

Einhorn, Hallie.
    Foyers & entryways / Hallie Einhorn.
         p.   cm. — (For your home)
    Includes index.
    ISBN 1-56799-449-0 (pbk.)
    1. Entrance halls. 2. Interior decoration. I. Title.
II. Series.
NK2117.E5E37 1997
747.7—dc20   96-36519
                                           CIP

Editors: Francine Hornberger and Reka Simonsen
Art Director: Lynne Yeamans
Layout: Robbi Firestone
Photography Editor: Wendy Missan
Production Manager: Camille Lee

Color separations by Fine Arts Repro House Co., Ltd.
Printed in Hong Kong by Midas Printing Limited

For bulk purchases and special sales, please contact:
Friedman/Fairfax Publishers
Attention: Sales Department
15 West 26th Street
New York, New York 10010
212/685-6610 FAX 212/685-1307

Visit our Website:
http://www.metrobooks.com

Table of Contents

Introduction ◼ 6

Architectural Details ◼ 10

The Power of Paint ◼ 28

Small Salutations ◼ 42

Grand Entrances ◼ 58

Sources ◼ 70

Index ◼ 72

Introduction

Like the opening scene of a play, the foyer sets the stage for what is to come. It introduces the tone of the rest of the decor, easing visitors through the transition of coming from their home to yours.

Entries appear in all shapes and sizes, though most are relatively small. But regardless of size, an entry can take on an infinite number of demeanors. The space can be decked out in a contemporary, traditional, ethnic, or eclectic fashion, though the chosen look is usually in keeping with the general style of the home. Mood can vary from casual and relaxed to cheerful and flamboyant or formal and dignified. As with any other room in the home, the decorative spectrum is vast. Setting the right mood is especially important in the entry, since this is the space from which visitors will glean their first impression of the residence.

There are a number of ways to ensure that the first impression is favorable. One way is to include a distinctive piece of furniture, such as a hand-painted console table or an offbeat coat rack. Another way is to incorporate an unusual paint treatment, such as a trompe l'oeil design. But most importantly, the entry should say something about the people who reside in the home. This space offers the perfect chance to display favorite objects and express personality, so take advantage of it and follow your instincts.

During the course of designing an entry, many practical considerations must be taken into account along with the decorative aspects. Because the foyer receives heavy traffic, the flooring material should be capable of withstanding wear and tear. It is a good idea to place a mat just outside the front door in order to reduce the amount of moisture and dirt tracked into the home. For added insurance, a mat or small area rug can be situated on the interior side of the doorway as well.

Such timeless naturals as stone and marble are good choices for entryway floors, since their hard surfaces are easily wiped clean and they are impervious to water. Similarly, tile tends to be toward the top of the list because of its low-maintenance nature and water-resistant properties. Hardwood is a favorite, too, valued for its classic look and its

Opposite: IN THIS SMALL ENTRY, A WEATHERED PAINTED CUPBOARD RADIATING RUSTIC CHARM NOT ONLY PROVIDES ATTRACTIVE STORAGE SPACE BUT ALSO SERVES AS THE BASE FOR A PICTURESQUE VIGNETTE. A BOWL OF FRUIT, A CERAMIC PITCHER FILLED WITH COLORFUL FLOWERS, AND A FEW TREASURED COLLECTIBLES ARE THE SIMPLE INGREDIENTS THAT MAKE UP THIS HIGHLY APPEALING STILL LIFE. FRAMED PRINTS AND A SMALL MIRROR MAKE WISE USE OF THE WALL SPACE BENEATH THE STAIRS, WHILE ORNATE WROUGHT-IRON BALUSTERS ADD VISUAL RHYTHM.

ability to stand up to scuffs and scratches. And thanks to up-grades in design and color, durable vinyl is also joining the ranks of materials appropriate for greeting guests.

Although not as easily maintained as the aforementioned materials, carpeting is also an option. Thanks to advances in stain-resistant treatments, textiles are becoming increasingly able to meet the demands of heavy traffic areas. While not as practical as stone, marble, and tile, carpeting does offer bonuses, such as its ability to reduce noise, its softening effect upon a room, and its deftness at hiding dust. If you do choose to use carpeting in an entry, be sure to obtain the highest quality possible.

Lighting is another crucial aspect of the foyer. Capable of altering the mood and contributing to the ambience, light can help set the tone of an entry, from boldly theatrical to softly romantic. Sidelights and transoms allow natural light to spill into the foyer, while such artificial alternatives as recessed lights, chandeliers, and uplights can take over in the absence

Above: In this modest-size entry, a narrow bookcase is situated against the wall, creating a home for an overflow of books while at the same time presenting an intellectual distraction for guests. Refusing to let any precious space go unused, a low-slung leather chair occupies the corner by the door, fitting squarely beneath the sidelight so as not to block the sun.

of daylight. Spotlights can be used to accentuate certain areas or decorative objects, while sconces can visually increase the height of the space by tossing light up onto the ceiling. By combining several different lighting techniques, a dramatic interplay of light and shadows can be achieved.

Lighting also promotes safety, which is of the utmost importance in an area where people are always coming and going. If a staircase is present, it should be well lit and there should be switches at both the bottom and top of the stairs. To further reduce the risk of tripping, the stair treads themselves can be lit as well.

In order to meet the needs of visitors and residents, a foyer should provide a spot for people to place keys, mail, gloves, and packages upon entering. Console tables are an ideal solution, especially since they come in narrow widths suitable for entries. Some creative alternatives include wall-mounted shelving, which is highly useful when space is at a premium, and a chest of drawers that is no longer needed in a bedroom.

Storage space for coats and umbrellas is also required. Ideally, a foyer will be graced with a closet, but have no fear if this is not the case. Coat racks and umbrella stands are space-efficient substitutes. Hooks and wall-hung shelves will also do the trick.

In the name of hospitality, it is important to have a place for visitors to sit. This way they can make themselves comfortable when arriving or preparing to depart. A simple chair or bench is sufficient in a small space, while in a larger foyer, you may wish to incorporate a sofa. A mirror will also be greatly appreciated by both guests and members of the household, for it offers the opportunity to quickly check one's hair, makeup, and general appearance. Moreover, mirrors can do wonders for the look of an entry by heightening the play of light and visually enlarging the space.

When all is said and done, an entry should be welcoming. While revealing a personal sense of style, it should also encourage everyone who passes through to feel at home.

Architectural Details

Since entries tend to have few pieces of furniture because of space constraints, these rooms provide the perfect opportunity for architectural embellishments to bask in the spotlight. In return for their moment of glory, such details imbue the entries they adorn with style and character, making these spaces worthy preludes to the rest of the home.

contemporary demeanor, while richly hued paneled doors provide a grounding sense of tradition. A double-door entrance, regardless of its design, will exude an air of grandeur.

Even more options come into play with regard to the area surrounding the door. Transoms and sidelights can take on any number of different shapes and sizes, while at the same time providing the highly practical service of ushering in natural light. On the purely decorative side, small carved details, such as rosettes, can appear in the corners of the door frame for added embellishment. Such simple touches often make lasting impressions.

The one element that all entries have in common is the door. But thanks to the abundance of architectural styles, from Georgian to Victorian to postmodern, doors appear in a wide variety of incarnations, giving each entry its own individual look. Flush doors present a cool, crisp,

Opposite: A MASSIVE FRONT DOOR WITH A RICH MAHOGANY FINISH PRESIDES OVER THIS MODERN FOYER. BRASS HARDWARE AND A GLASS-BLOCK SIDELIGHT ACCENTUATE THE ENTRANCE, WHILE GRAY CARPETING HEIGHTENS THE SPACE'S COMMANDING TONE. **Above:** EMBELLISHING STAIR RISERS WITH HAND-PAINTED TILES IS A SIMPLE WAY OF SPICING UP AN ENTRY. HERE, JUST A FEW COLORFUL TILES JAZZ UP THE TERRA-COTTA PAVED STEPS LEADING FROM THE FRONT DOOR TO THE REST OF THE HOME. AS GUESTS DEPART, THE BRIGHT RISERS STAND OUT AGAINST THE EARTHY TREADS, ANNOUNCING THE CHANGE IN LEVELS.

Once visitors and residents have crossed the threshold, a host of different architectural details can step forward to entertain. Cornices, chair rails, dadoes, and paneling break up the monotony of flat walls, urging the eye to peruse the space from floor to ceiling. If a staircase is present, its balustrade can be incorporated into the decorative mix so as to contribute to the overall mood. Wrought-iron balusters with intricate detailing can invoke the feeling of a Spanish villa, while a railing with swirling lines can create a fanciful look. Best of all, these beautiful results can be achieved without eating up valuable space.

Below: TWO VAST DOORWAYS SERVE AS MIRROR IMAGES OF EACH OTHER IN THIS DIGNIFIED YET CHEERFUL FOYER. THE SECOND SET OF DOORS OPENS ONTO A COURTYARD THAT CAN ALWAYS BE RELISHED FROM WITHIN THROUGH THE FULL-LENGTH GLASS PANES, WHICH PROVIDE AN UNOBSTRUCTED VIEW. IDENTICAL TOPIARIES JUST OUTSIDE THE FRONT DOOR HERALD THE SYMMETRY THAT LIES ACROSS THE THRESHOLD.

Opposite: A FANLIGHT AND GLASS PANEL, BOTH BEARING SUBTLE BLUE TINTS, GIVE THIS ENTRANCE A BREEZY FEELING. FRENCH DOORS MAINTAIN THE AIRY SENSATION AND ALLOW THE COLORFUL GLASS ARTWORK TO REMAIN IN VIEW WHEN THE ANTEROOM IS CLOSED OFF. **Above:** LEADED GLASS IMBUES THIS ENTRANCE WITH A TRADITIONAL FLAVOR THAT IS REINFORCED BY A WROUGHT-IRON ESCUTCHEON AND WHITE SLAT PANELING. THE SHAPES OF THE GLASS FEATURES ARE REMINISCENT OF CATHEDRAL WINDOWS, GIVING THE SPACE A GOTHIC FEELING. SO THAT THE TWO RADIATORS FLANKING THE DOORWAY DO NOT DETRACT FROM THE PRETTY PICTURE, THEY HAVE BEEN TRANSFORMED INTO UNOBTRUSIVE DISPLAY STANDS, THEIR GRATING SLYLY CONCEALED BY A TUB OF FLOWERS AND A LARGE WICKER BASKET.

Below: ALTHOUGH THE EVOCATIVE ARCHED WINDOW LYING BEHIND THIS SPANISH COLONIAL REVIVAL DOOR IS A BEAUTIFUL DECORATIVE ASSET, IT UNFORTUNATELY CAUSES THE SMALL SPACE TO HEAT UP QUICKLY ON SUMMER DAYS. DURING SUCH TIMES, A YELLOW ROD-HUNG CURTAIN COMES TO THE RESCUE, BLOCKING HARSH RAYS WHILE MAINTAINING A SUNNY LOOK. **Opposite:** LARGE PANES OF GLASS ON THE FRONT DOOR ALLOW PLENTY OF LIGHT TO STREAM INTO THIS VAST FOYER. A SPIRAL STAIRCASE DRAWS THE EYE UP TO THE SKY, WHILE A COUPLE OF WELL-PLACED BEAMS SEEK TO CONTAIN THE SPACE. AN OVERWHELMING SENSE OF UNITY PERVADES THE GROUND FLOOR, THANKS TO THE PRESENCE OF WHITE WALLS AND DARK WOODEN FLOORS IN EACH ROOM.

Above: THE UNEXPECTED COMBINATION OF CURVING WALLS AND SQUARE PANELS GREETS VISITORS WITH A REFRESHING SENSE OF CONTRAST. WHILE TWO AREA RUGS ECHO THE LINES OF THE UNDULATING WALLS, THE STAIRCASE REFLECTS THE ANGULAR NATURE OF THE PANELS. THE GLASS-PANELED DOOR LEADING FROM THE FOYER TO THE DEN LETS LIGHT SHINE THROUGH INTO THIS MODERN ENTRY.

Below: AN ARCHED TRANSOM WITH WEBLIKE TRACERY SURMOUNTS A DARK PANELED DOOR TO LEND IT AN AIR OF IMPORTANCE. THE DOOR'S RICH HUE AND BRASS HARDWARE GIVE THE ENTRANCE A TRADITIONAL TONE THAT IS HEIGHTENED BY CHIPPENDALE FURNISHINGS AND A PAIR OF ORIENTAL RUGS. TOGETHER, THESE ELEMENTS CREATE A STATELY ENTRANCE THAT MAINTAINS A RESERVED RATHER THAN EXTRAVAGANT DISPOSITION. HOWEVER, A CURLICUE MOLDING DANCING WHIMSICALLY ALONG THE LOWER PORTION OF THE STAIRS REVEALS THAT THIS HOME IS NOT ABOVE HAVING A BIT OF FUN.

Opposite: ADOBE WALLS, TERRA-COTTA TILES, A PROFUSE ARRANGEMENT OF FOLIAGE, AND AN ABUNDANCE OF SUNLIGHT GIVE THIS SOUTHWESTERN ENTRYWAY THE AMBIENCE OF A PATIO. INTRICATE CARVINGS ON THE DOUBLE-DOOR ENTRANCE PROVIDE A COMPELLING DIVERSION FROM THE SMOOTH SURFACES OF THE SURROUNDING WALLS, WHILE FESTIVE PAINTS ON THE BENCH AND PLANT STAND INJECT THE NEUTRAL PALETTE WITH HEALTHY DOSES OF COLOR. A WAVY CEILING, WHICH PROVIDES A FOIL FOR THE FLAT TILES BELOW, INVOKES THE IMAGE OF A RIPPLING AWNING.

Above: THE SIMPLICITY OF THIS FRONT DOOR IS ECHOED BY COLONIAL FURNISHINGS AND A BASIC CHECKERBOARD FLOOR. TO EMPHASIZE THE FORMALITY OF THE ADJOINING LIVING ROOM, AN AUTHORITATIVE PEDIMENT MARKS THE PASSAGE LEADING TO IT.

Above: BECAUSE THIS ENTRY HAS NO WINDOWS OTHER THAN A SLIM SIDELIGHT, THE SPACE TENDS TO BE DARK. TO BRING IN ADDITIONAL LIGHT, THE INNER PANELED DOOR IS LEFT OPEN SO THAT AN OUTER DOOR FITTED WITH A SHEET OF PLAIN GLASS CAN USHER IN THE SUN. WHEN NIGHT FALLS OR PRIVACY IS DESIRED, THE INNER DOOR CAN BE SHUT FOR HEIGHTENED SECURITY. THE PALE HUES OF THE ENTRY'S WALLS, FLOOR, AND BENCH HELP TO KEEP THE SPACE LIGHT AND UPLIFTING. **Opposite:** A LOG BALUSTRADE HELPS MAINTAIN THE NATURAL LOOK OF THIS MOUNTAIN RETREAT. UNLIKE TRADITIONAL BANISTERS, WHICH TEND TO HAVE SLEEK PROFILES, THE RAILING IS RIFE WITH CROOKED LINES, CREATING A RUSTIC TONE THAT IS HIGHLY APPROPRIATE FOR THE SETTING. AN AREA RUG WITH A SOUTHWESTERN FLAVOR CASUALLY SETS OFF THE ENTRANCE FROM THE REST OF THE LIVING SPACE.

Left: This foyer's stunning doorway, with its rounded top and many-paned frame, is typical of Arts and Crafts design. The hanging light fixture and checkerboard marble floor are in keeping with this elegant style, but a few contemporary elements, such as the angular console table and the sculptures, have been blended in to great effect.

Opposite: The classical beauty of this foyer is emphasized by the simplicity of its decor. The rectangular columns and geometric tiled floor are reminiscent of ancient Greece, while the porcelain vases by the door hail from the Far East. Potted ivy plants bring a touch of the outdoors inside.

Opposite: INSTEAD OF INDIVIDUAL BALUSTERS, SOLID WOOD IS USED TO SUPPORT THE HANDRAIL OF THIS STAIRCASE, CREATING A SLEEK LOOK THAT SUITS THE CONTEMPORARY SURROUNDINGS. THE GRAINING ON THE UNUSUAL BANISTER ECHOES THE SLOPE OF THE STAIRS. BECAUSE THE ENTRY HAS A GENEROUS AMOUNT OF SPACE, THE OWNERS HAVE TAKEN THE OPPORTUNITY TO USE IT AS AN EXHIBITION HALL, DISPLAYING ARTWORK, A STATUE, AND A COLLECTION OF CERAMIC POTTERY. **Above, left:** THE GLASS PANES OF THIS FRONT DOOR ALLOW THE BEAUTY OF AN OUTSIDE COURTYARD TO BE ENJOYED FROM WITHIN THE VESTIBULE. TO MAINTAIN A SENSE OF HARMONY BETWEEN THE TWO WORLDS, THE DOOR FRAME AND MULLIONS HAVE BEEN PAINTED A MINTY SHADE OF GREEN THAT MATCHES THE OUTDOOR FURNITURE. A SMALL STAINED GLASS WINDOW PROVIDES ILLUMINATION FOR THE STAIRS, CASTING A SOFT RED GLOW THAT IS ECHOED BY A SIMPLE YET BOLD VASE. **Above, right:** TWO MASSIVE DORIC COLUMNS STAND AS SENTRIES MARKING THE BORDER BETWEEN THE FOYER AND LIVING ROOM. KEEPING VIGILANT WATCH OVER THOSE WHO CROSS INTO THE HEART OF THE HOME, THEY CREATE THE IMPRESSION THAT SOMETHING PRECIOUS LIES BEYOND THEM.

Below: IN THIS ELEGANTLY UNDERSTATED ENTRYWAY, A DYNAMIC GRID-PATTERNED BALUSTRADE INSTANTLY CAPTURES THE EYE. A CRISP WHITE COAT OF PAINT KEEPS ATTENTION FOCUSED ON THE GRID, WHILE SOFT SEA-FOAM WALLS PROVIDE A SUBTLE BACKDROP. CURVACEOUS VASES OFFER A PLEASANT COUNTER-POINT TO THE STAIRCASE'S FORCEFUL LINES, PREVENTING THE ENTRY FROM SEEMING TOO AUSTERE. **Opposite:** THIS SPECTACULAR STAIRCASE BRANCHES OFF INTO TWO DIFFERENT SEGMENTS THAT RESEMBLE OUTSTRETCHED ARMS READY TO EMBRACE AND GREET VISITORS. RUNNERS MIRROR THE SYMMETRY OF THE STAIRS WHILE POINTING OUT THE VARIOUS DIRECTIONS THAT GUESTS CAN TAKE. A PAIR OF GLOBES STANDING ON EITHER SIDE OF THE ARCHWAY SUGGEST THAT THERE ARE AN INFINITE AMOUNT OF POSSIBLE DESTINATIONS.

Above: PURE ARCHITECTURAL STYLING IS RESPONSIBLE FOR THE STRIKING STATEMENT MADE BY THIS ENTRANCE. BY INCORPORATING PANES OF VARYING SHAPES AND SIZES INTO ITS DESIGN, THE ENORMOUS GLASS ARRANGEMENT IS BROKEN DOWN INTO SMALLER SECTIONS THAT CAN EASILY BE TAKEN IN BY THE EYE. SO AS NOT TO BE OUTDONE BY THE ARRESTING CONFIGURATION, THE FLOOR HAS BEEN CARPETED IN A BRILLIANT SHADE OF TURQUOISE.

Left: ARCHITECTURAL DETAILS TAKE THE PLACE OF HANGING ART IN THIS EXQUISITE ENTRY. SMALL SQUARE PANES WITH THICK WHITE CASINGS FRAME THE DOOR, CREATING AN EYE-CATCHING GRID. BULLSEYE WINDOWS POSSESSING THE SAME WHITE TRIM POP UP ON EITHER SIDE, OFFERING A SOFT COUNTERPOINT TO THE RECTANGULAR DOOR FRAME. THE ENTIRE ARRANGEMENT EXUDES CLASSICAL SYMMETRY, WHICH IS CARRIED THROUGH IN THE LIVING ROOM BY THE PRECISE, EVEN PLACE-MENT OF FOUR ARMCHAIRS AROUND A CIRCULAR TABLE. **Above:** AT NIGHT, THE ENTRY'S FENESTRATION PRESENTS A SPEC-TACULAR LIGHT SHOW, GENERATING A WAVE OF EXCITEMENT BEFORE VISITORS EVEN ENTER THE HOME.

THE POWER OF PAINT

With its almost magical powers of illusion and camouflage, paint can transform a space. A light hue can make a small foyer seem larger, while a vibrant shade can brighten up a dark entry. And thanks to more intricate treatments, such as faux finishes and trompe l'oeil designs, walls and floors are able to take on convincing new personalities at relatively reasonable costs.

Like architectural details, paint can enhance an entry when space constraints prevent furnishings from doing the trick. Unexpected colors and combinations will delight the eye just as much as an unusual piece of furniture or a collection of objets d'art. Bathing an entry in a single dynamic color makes a striking statement, but accenting details in contrasting colors can be just as exciting.

Of course, the paint treatment needn't be the main attraction of an entry. Indeed, paint often provides a subtle but nonetheless vital background for comfortable furnishings and treasured collectibles on display. A faux marble treatment on ordinary walls, for example, can provide a captivating focal point or a stunning backdrop. Either way, it exudes opulence.

It is paint's ability to evoke a mood that makes it an asset in the foyer. Warm colors convey energy and vitality, while cool colors offer serenity and can help lend a contemporary look. A faux stone treatment on walls and flooring can transport visitors back in time, while something as simple as a stenciled border can impart a country feeling. The possibilities are endless.

Opposite: A STUDY IN CONTRASTS, THIS MULTITONED STAINED FLOOR BOASTS ELABORATE SWIRLING STENCILED DESIGNS INTERSPERSED WITH SIMPLE, ANGULAR GEOMETRIC SHAPES. THE STRONG, DARK HUES ARE COUNTERBALANCED BY PALE YELLOW WALLS AND WHITE TRIM, BOTH OF WHICH HAVE A TAMING EFFECT UPON THE UNABASHEDLY WILD FLOOR. **Above:** BECAUSE THIS ENTRY AFFORDS LITTLE SPACE FOR HANGING ART, THE DESIGNER INGENIOUSLY TRANSFORMED A CLOSET DOOR INTO TWO PAINTINGS. EACH OF THE SLIGHTLY INSET PANELS SERVES AS A CANVAS. A TOUCHING PASTORAL SCENE GRACES THE TOP PORTION OF THE DOOR, WHILE A CHEERY STILL LIFE "HANGS" BELOW. AS THE ARTWORK TAKES CENTER STAGE, A PRACTICAL SLATE FLOOR AND MINIMALIST WOOD BENCH GRACIOUSLY WAIT IN THE WINGS, READY TO PERFORM THEIR HUMBLE SERVICES AT A MOMENT'S NOTICE.

Above: WITH A FLAIR FOR THE DRAMATIC, THE DESIGNER OF THIS HOME PAINTED THE ENTIRE ENTRYWAY—WALLS, FLOOR, STAIRS, BANISTER, AND DOOR—RED. EVEN SUCH DETAILS AS THE WINDOW CASING, MULLIONS, AND DOOR HINGES ARE COVERED IN THIS VIBRANT HUE. BECAUSE THE EXTENSIVE USE OF RED IS SO POWERFUL, FURNISHINGS HAVE BEEN KEPT TO A MINIMUM. A CHAIR UPHOLSTERED IN RED LEATHER IS POSITIONED BY THE DOOR SO VISITORS CAN REST WEARY FEET. **Right:** DEEP BLUE PAINT INFUSES THIS SPACIOUS ENTRY WITH A SENSE OF DRAMA THAT IS PLAYED UP BY WALL-WASHING RECESSED LIGHTS. SANDWICHED BETWEEN A WHITE CORNICE AND DADO, THE STRIKING HUE PROVIDES EXHILARATING CONTRAST AND SUGGESTS A SENSE OF DARING ON THE PART OF THE OWNERS. FURTHER EVIDENCE OF SUCH DECORATING BRAVADO IS SEEN IN THE PLACEMENT OF A STRIPED RUNNER ATOP A CHECKERBOARD TILE FLOOR, A BRAZEN COMBINATION THAT IMPLIES ADDITIONAL CONVENTION-DEFYING ARRANGEMENTS AWAIT IN THE ROOMS BEYOND.

Above: EVER THE MASTER OF ILLUSION, PAINT SERVES AS AN ARTFUL STAND-IN FOR MORE EXPENSIVE MATERIALS. HERE, WOODEN FLOORBOARDS ARE TRANSFORMED INTO ELEGANT "TILES," THANKS TO A FAUX MARBLE TREATMENT. ON THE STAIRS, A CLEVER PAINT JOB CREATES A WORRY-FREE RUNNER THAT DOES NOT HAVE TO BE TACKED DOWN LIKE TEXTILE VERSIONS. AND LAST BUT NOT LEAST, A STENCILED DESIGN JUST BELOW THE CORNICE TAKES THE PLACE OF A WALLPAPER BORDER, IMBUING THE ENTRYWAY WITH HOMESPUN CHARM. **Opposite:** SINCE THIS VESTIBULE IS TOO SMALL TO BE FURNISHED WITH ANYTHING MORE THAN A CHAIR, PAINT PROVIDES THE VISUAL INTEREST. A BREATHTAKING LAVENDER HUE SELDOM SEEN ON WALLS PRESENTS THOSE WHO ENTER WITH A PLEASANT SURPRISE. MEANWHILE, WHITE PAINT—USED ON THE DOORS, TRIM, AND CEILING—EXERTS A PRISTINE INFLUENCE, ALLOWING THE VESTIBULE TO MAINTAIN AN INNOCENT RATHER THAN RADICAL LOOK. DAINTY LACE CURTAINS REINFORCE THE SENSE OF PROPRIETY, WHILE SIMULTANEOUSLY OBSCURING THE VIEW OF NOSY NEIGHBORS.

Opposite: A SUNNY SHADE OF YELLOW KEEPS THIS ENTRY LOOKING SUMMERY THROUGHOUT THE SEASONS. WHITE PAINT ACCENTS THE SPACE AND CALLS ATTENTION TO THE ABUNDANCE OF ARCHITECTURAL DETAILS, WHICH INCLUDE A VARIETY OF PICTURE RAILS, A DAZZLING ARRAY OF CLOSELY SPACED BALUSTERS, AND MOLDING THAT TRACES THE SLOPE OF THE STAIRS. MEANWHILE, DEEP BLUE CURTAINS, A BLUE VASE, AND A PREDOMINANTLY BLUE UMBRELLA STAND PUNCTUATE THE AIRY ENTRANCE WITH A GROUNDING SENSE OF DEPTH. **Below:** THE COOL HUES OF THIS ENTRYWAY MAKE IT A HAVEN ON WARM SUMMER DAYS. WHITE TRIM ADDS TO THE TRANQUILITY, WHILE A RED TABLECLOTH AND HAND-PAINTED BENCH SERVE AS BUOYANT ACCENTS.

Above: OUTLINED IN BLACK AND GOLD, THE EXTERIOR OF THIS FRONT DOOR ECHOES THE COLOR SCHEME OF THE FOYER, PROVIDING VISITORS WITH A CLUE AS TO WHAT THE INTERIOR HAS IN STORE FOR THEM. ONCE INSIDE, GUESTS ARE ENVELOPED IN THE HEARTENING AUTUMN GLOW EMANATING FROM THE SPACE'S PALETTE, WHICH IS REMINISCENT OF THE WREATH HANGING OUTSIDE. ARCHITECTURAL ELEMENTS, NAMELY WALL PANELS AND AN ORNAMENTAL PILASTER, ARE DECKED PRIMARILY IN BLACK SO AS TO STAND OUT AGAINST THE GOLDEN BACKGROUND.

Opposite: TO CREATE A VITAL SENSE OF CONTRAST WITH THE NEUTRAL-COLORED WALLS OF THIS ENTRANCE, THE ARCHITECTURAL TRIM WAS PAINTED FOREST GREEN. THE COLOR ECHOES THE DENSE FOLIAGE OF THE SURROUNDING LANDSCAPE, WHICH IS HIGHLY VISIBLE INDOORS THANKS TO LARGE SIDELIGHTS AND FRENCH DOORS. AN AREA RUG IN AN INTENSE SHADE OF RED COMPLEMENTS THE GREEN HUE AND FURTHER INVIGORATES THE SPACE.

Above: A SPIRITED HEXAGONAL PATTERN PAINTED ON WOODEN FLOORBOARDS ENCOURAGES VISITORS TO STEP LIVELY. ALTERNATING BE-TWEEN BRIGHT WHITE HEXAGONS AND BEIGE ONES EMBELLISHED WITH RED VEINING, THE DESIGN ADDS A BIT OF ZEST TO THE SURROUNDING EARLY AMERICAN FURNISHINGS. BLUE PAINT HIGHLIGHTS THE CORNICES, THE TRIM AROUND THE TRANSOM OF THE FAR DOOR, AND THE MOLDING AROUND THE ARCH SITUATED IN THE MIDDLE OF THE PASSAGEWAY.

Right: IN ORDER TO ESTABLISH A CLEAR DISTINCTION BETWEEN THE ENTRANCE HALL AND LIVING ROOM, THE FLOORBOARDS IN THE FORMER WERE PAINTED TO RESEMBLE A TILED FLOOR GRACED BY A NEEDLEPOINT RUNNER. THE CHECKERBOARD ARRANGEMENT OF THE PAINTED "TILES" PROVIDES A CLASSIC TOUCH THAT BLENDS IN WELL WITH THE TRADITIONAL FURNISHINGS AND PAINTED URN. MEANWHILE, THE TURNED-UP CORNER OF A TROMPE L'OEIL RUNNER INTRODUCES A BIT OF SARCASM, MOCKING THE PROBLEMS OF ITS TEXTILE COUNTERPARTS.

Above: By using staining techniques, the designer of this foyer has created a sheer runner of sorts, allowing the natural graining of the floorboards to remain visible. The rapidly repeating pattern of the stenciled border suggests movement, appropriate for this heavy traffic area, while two cheerful bouquets invite guests to linger a moment longer. The space under the console table is wisely used to display an antique birdcage.

Above: When there is not much room for furniture, an imaginative paint job can serve as a refreshing decorative substitute. Here, a trompe l'oeil display cabinet gives its owners the opportunity to show off any treasures their hearts desire. Paint also plays a crucial role on the wide floorboards, which, with their olive and ocher checkerboard pattern, imbue the room with a country feeling. Thanks to louvered panels and sidelights, an abundance of natural light floods the room during daylight hours.

Above: Painted vines and flowers heighten the earthy tone of this entry. Defying the compactness of the space, the vines are large and dense, refusing to be contained. The untamed look of the foliage reflects the primitive nature of the objects on display. **Opposite:** Burnt sienna brings the radiance of a sunset to this narrow entry. While the original gray hue of the walls made the steep staircase rather daunting, the new color stimulates the senses and encourages visitors to press onward. An array of small windows helps to brighten up the space.

SMALL SALUTATIONS

As the saying goes, "Good things come in small packages." The same holds true for small entryways. Although not big in size, these spaces can be big in heart, embracing visitors with hospitality and welcoming them into the home.

One way to make a small or medium-size entryway inviting is by incorporating a few prized possessions or favorite collectibles into the decor. Reflective of the host's character, such decorative objects infuse the space with personal charm. Console tables are perfect for showcasing these special items, which can be arranged to form a charming vignette. Wall-hung shelves and display niches are other space-efficient and flattering means of showing off a collection of sentimental treasures.

Along the same lines, hanging artwork can be used to liven up a small entry. A wall can be peppered with an array of small prints or covered with a spectacular painting that practically fills up the entire surface. And do not forget the wall space under the stairs, which can be a prime location for displaying a favorite work of art.

But a small entry does not have to include purely decorative components. If space is used resourcefully, a cozy sitting area or an efficient work spot can be created. Of course, the furnishings used to fashion these areas combine with the flooring, lighting, and decorative objects to set the mood. Whether the tone is traditional, southwestern, or modern, each entrance has its own special way of saying "hello."

Opposite: A LOVE OF CLASSICAL ARCHITECTURE INSPIRED THE WALLPAPER FOR THIS ENTRANCE HALL. TO MAKE THE FORMERLY PLAIN WOODEN FLOORBOARDS WORTHY OF SUCH GRAND COMPANY, A GLOSSY FINISH WAS APPLIED OVER PAINTED-ON BLACK AND WHITE DIAMONDS. A GILT MIRROR, FLANKED BY SIMPLE SCONCES THAT COMPLEMENT RATHER THAN COMPETE WITH IT, PROVIDES A POSH TOUCH. **Above:** THIS SIMPLE YET EFFICIENT ENTRY IS HIGHLY CONSIDERATE OF GUESTS AND RESIDENTS ALIKE. A WOODEN CHAIR UPHOLSTERED IN PLAID PROVIDES A COMFORTABLE PLACE TO REST WHILE WAITING TO GO OUT; A FULL-LENGTH MIRROR FREE OF ELABORATE DETAILING OFFERS THE OPPORTUNITY TO PRIMP; A SIDE TABLE WELCOMES KEYS AND MAIL; AND A PORCELAIN STAND WITH AN ORIENTAL FLAVOR READILY RECEIVES UMBRELLAS. PETITE FRAMED PRINTS OF DELICATE BIRDS ASCEND WITH THE STAIRS, PROVIDING AN EYE-CATCHING DIVERSION FOR THOSE JOURNEYING UP AND DOWN.

Above: GLOSSY BLACK AND WHITE TILES GIVE THIS SMALL VESTIBULE THE ELEGANCE OF A GRAND FOYER. REINFORCING THE REFINED LOOK ARE AN ANTIQUE MARBLE-TOPPED TABLE AND SOFT COVE LIGHTING. A VINTAGE POSTER HANGS MAJESTICALLY AT THE FAR END OF THE HALL, COAXING VISITORS TO VENTURE FARTHER INTO THE HOME.

Below: SINCE THERE IS NO ROOM FOR FURNITURE IN THIS NARROW ENTRYWAY, THE DESIGNER DECIDED TO CAPITALIZE UPON THE VAST AMOUNT OF WALL SPACE. CREATING A GALLERY OF SORTS, A PRIZED COLLECTION OF MASKS WAS HUNG IN AN ORDERLY ROW ALONG THE CORRIDOR THAT LEADS TO THE REST OF THE FIRST FLOOR. EACH MASK IS SHOWN OFF TO ADVANTAGE, THANKS TO THE INDIVIDUAL WALL PANEL THAT FRAMES IT. THE LOFTY POSITION OF THE ENSEMBLE ALLOWS IT TO BE ENJOYED BY PEOPLE ASCENDING THE STAIRS AS WELL AS THOSE WHO REMAIN AT GROUND LEVEL.

Above: A DEFT HAND CAN CREATE THE FEELING OF AN ENTRYWAY EVEN WHEN THE FRONT DOOR OPENS DIRECTLY ONTO THE LIVING ROOM. THE SECRET LIES IN THE LAYOUT. HERE, ANGLING A CHAIR TOWARD THE DOORWAY AND AWAY FROM THE SITTING AREA CREATES A NEW FOCUS. TWO AREA RUGS—ONE IN PALE SHADES OF BLUE AND BEIGE, THE OTHER SPORTING TOUCHES OF DEEP RED—ALSO HELP TO PULL OFF THE EFFECT. WHILE ONE OUTLINES THE BOUNDARIES OF THE LIVING ROOM, THE OTHER DEFINES THE ENTRANCE. A WOODEN UMBRELLA STAND FILLED WITH AN ASSORTMENT OF ANTIQUE CANES AND PLACED BY THE DOOR FURTHER CONTRIBUTES TO THE ENTRYWAY AMBIENCE.

Above: BECKONING VISITORS TO REST AND RELAX, SUMPTUOUS UPHOLSTERED ARMCHAIRS FLANKING A ROUND WOODEN TABLE PROMOTE HOSPITALITY AND ENCOURAGE QUIET CONVERSATION. THE COZY SETUP, WARMED BY A RICHLY HUED ORIENTAL RUG AND A VASE OF FRESH FLOWERS, IS MUCH MORE INTIMATE THAN THE VAST LIVING ROOM THAT LIES OFF TO THE SIDE AND THUS PROVIDES A MORE DESIRABLE SPOT FOR A TÊTE-À-TÊTE. **Opposite:** THE SPACE BENEATH A SWIRLING STAIRCASE BECOMES THE IDEAL LOCATION FOR A READING NOOK. WITH THE STAIRS OVERHEAD SERVING AS A CANOPY OF SORTS, A SNUG ALCOVE IS CREATED. FURNISHED WITH AN INVITING UPHOLSTERED WING CHAIR THAT IS PERFECT FOR CURLING UP IN, A SLENDER FLOOR LAMP THAT PROVIDES DIRECT LIGHT FOR READING, AND A MAHOGANY SIDE TABLE THAT OFFERS A RESTING SPOT FOR BOOKS, THE AREA HAS A HIGHLY TRADITIONAL TONE. A SPRAWLING PLANT PROVIDES A SOFTENING TOUCH, FILLING UP WHAT WOULD OTHERWISE BE A DARK, FOREBODING CORNER.

Below: EVEN BACK ENTRANCES MERIT DECORATIVE ATTENTION. ALTHOUGH THESE PASSAGEWAYS MAY NOT BE FREQUENTED BY GUESTS, THEY ARE TRAVELED HEAVILY BY RESIDENTS, WHO DESERVE TO HAVE APPEALING SURROUNDINGS. HERE, QUAINT BASKETS DANGLE FROM THE CEILING BEAMS TO PROVIDE VISUAL ENTERTAINMENT OVERHEAD, WHILE AN ASSORTMENT OF GLASS JARS USED FOR PICKLING AND PRESERVING INJECTS A COUNTRY FLAVOR CLOSER TO EYE-LEVEL. PRACTICAL ELEMENTS INCLUDE A FLAGSTONE FLOOR, WHICH STANDS UP WELL TO MUD AND DIRT, AND A WOODEN CANISTER USED TO STORE SPORTS EQUIPMENT.

Above: BOASTING AN ABUNDANCE OF GREENERY AND A TERRA-COTTA TILE FLOOR, THIS NARROW ENTRY RESEMBLES AN ENCLOSED PORCH. SKY BLUE WALLS HELP TO BRING THE FEELING OF THE OUTDOORS INSIDE, WHILE A ROW OF GENEROUSLY SIZED WINDOWS USHERS IN NATURAL LIGHT. DURING TIMES WHEN THE SUN IS NOT SHEDDING ITS RAYS UPON THIS SIDE OF THE HOUSE, SCONCES PLACED CLOSE TO THE CEILING THROW THEIR LIGHT UPWARDS AND CAST A WARM GLOW OVER THE SPACE.

Below: A WICKER SIDE TABLE, A PAINTED-WHITE CHAIR, AND A BOX STUDDED WITH SEASHELLS REINFORCE THE BEACH THEME OF THIS SEASIDE RETREAT. SCULPTURAL WOODEN FLOWERS PAINTED IN TROPICAL COLORS REMAIN IN FULL BLOOM YEAR-ROUND, LIVENING UP THE SPACE WITH THEIR ETERNAL RADIANCE. A MIRROR HUNG ABOVE THE CHEERY VIGNETTE REFLECTS THE BACK OF THE TALLEST FLOWER, EXPOSING FANTASTICAL STRIPES THAT SUGGEST THE PRESENCE OF A WONDERLAND-TYPE WORLD THROUGH THE LOOKING GLASS.

Above: THE ECLECTIC COLLECTIONS OF THIS OCTAGONAL VESTIBULE CONTRIBUTE TO ITS OVERALL PROVINCIAL TONE. EMPHASIZING THE COUNTRY MOOD ARE A WHITE WICKER DISPLAY TABLE, AN ASSORTMENT OF BLUE AND WHITE CHINA PLATES HUNG ABOVE THE WINDOWS, AND RED AND WHITE SWAGS REMINISCENT OF PICNIC BLANKETS. A PALE WOOD CEILING PROVIDES WELCOME CONTRAST TO THE DEEP GREEN WALLS, EFFECTIVELY OPENING UP THE SPACE AND MAKING THE CEILING SEEM HIGHER. OVERHEAD, A CHARMING CHANDELIER RESEMBLING A HOT-AIR BALLOON FILLS THE ROOM WITH A SENSE OF ADVENTURE.

Opposite: A GLASS PEDESTAL TABLE BOASTING A LAVISH FLORAL ARRANGE-MENT IS THE FOCAL POINT IN THIS FOYER. A WHITE WINDOW TREATMENT ADDS TO THE UNDERSTATED ELEGANCE OF THE ROOM, WHILE A DIMINUTIVE CHAIR INJECTS CHILDLIKE WHIMSY. THE FOYER IS GRACED WITH A COPIOUS AMOUNT OF LIGHT THANKS TO SIDELIGHTS AND A LARGE WINDOW, THE LATTER BEING A RARITY IN ENTRANCE HALLS. **Below:** A RUSTIC SIDE TABLE PLAYS HOST TO AN ARRAY OF OFFBEAT OBJECTS, LENDING THIS ENTRY AN AIR OF QUIRKY CHARM. THE CEN-TERPIECE OF THE DIVERSE COLLECTION IS A LAMP FASHIONED FROM AN OLD URN, WHICH SERVES AS A DECORATIVE OBJECT AS WELL AS A SOURCE OF ILLUMINA-TION. BENEATH THE TABLE, A WOODEN BIN PROVIDES RESOURCEFUL STORAGE FOR SPORTS EQUIPMENT.

Above: WHAT WAS ONCE DULL EMPTY SPACE IS NOW A WARM, EYE-PLEASING SCENE THANKS TO A SIMPLE TABLE AND A FEW ACCOUTREMENTS. THE CURVING WALL AND BANISTER EMBRACE THE ROUNDNESS OF THE TABLE, WHICH NESTLES COMFORTABLY INTO THE NOOK AS THOUGH IT WERE BORN THERE.

Above: PAVED WITH TERRA-COTTA TILES, THIS ENTRY EMANATES A SOUTHWESTERN FLAVOR. WHILE SIMPLE SQUARE TILES LINE THE GROUND LEVEL, HEXAGONS AND TRAPEZOIDS GIVE THE STAIRS AN EXCITING EDGE. AREA RUGS IN SUBTLE SHADES OF RED, BLUE, AND BROWN ADD TEXTURE TO THE SETTING AND CUSHION THE FEET.

Opposite: WITH NO REAL FOYER TO SPEAK OF, THE FRONT DOOR OF THIS CABIN RETREAT OPENS DIRECTLY ONTO THE MAIN LIVING SPACE. IN ORDER TO CREATE A MUCH-NEEDED "CLOSET" FOR STORING SKIS AND BOOTS BESIDE THE ENTRANCE, A CURTAIN SECTIONING OFF A SMALL AREA WAS HUNG FROM A LOG BEAM. WITH ITS EARTHY HUES, THE TEXTILE PARTITION BLENDS WELL WITH ITS SURROUNDINGS WHILE AT THE SAME TIME HIDING THE STORAGE SPACE. SIMILAR CAMOUFLAGING TECHNIQUES CAN BE USED IN LESS RUSTIC SURROUNDINGS WITH THE HELP OF A CURTAIN OR FOLDING SCREEN THAT CORRESPONDS WITH THE DECOR.

Left: IN THIS MINUTE VESTIBULE, A SPACE-SAVING CORNER SHELF TAKES THE PLACE OF A CONSOLE TABLE. WITH PLENTY OF ROOM ABOVE AND BELOW IT, THE SIMPLE LEDGE MAINTAINS THE OPEN, AIRY FEELING ACHIEVED BY THE HOME'S PRIMARILY PALE PALETTE AND MINIMAL USE OF FURNISHINGS. A RED AND WHITE VASE OVERFLOWING WITH BOLD BLOOMS INTRODUCES A REFRESHING SPLASH OF COLOR TO THE NEUTRAL SURROUNDINGS, AS DOES A DYNAMIC YELLOW CHAIR VISIBLE IN THE LIVING ROOM BEYOND. **Opposite:** THE SUN ON THIS BEAUTIFULLY PAINTED FLOOR SEEMS TO OPEN UP THE SPACE AS ITS ENER-GETIC GOLDEN RAYS REACH OUT TOWARD THE ROOM'S BOUNDARIES, STRIVING TO EXCEED THEM. RED TONE-ON-TONE WALLPAPER BATHES THE VESTIBULE IN OPULENCE AND CONTRASTS RADIANTLY AGAINST THE LIGHTER HUES OF THE FLOOR AND MOLDINGS. A NECESSARY VENT, FORMERLY AN EYESORE, MINGLES UNOBTRU-SIVELY WITH THE REST OF THE DECOR, THANKS TO A CLEVER USE OF PAINT THAT ALLOWS THE DEVICE TO MELT INTO THE BASEBOARD.

Left: SPORTING A PRINT OF SHIPS AND MILLS, THE WALLPAPER IN THIS ENTRYWAY REFLECTS THE HOME'S NEW ENGLAND LOCALE. THE WHITE STAIR RISERS AND BALUSTERS LIGHTEN UP THE AREA, HELPING TO VISUALLY EXPAND THE SMALL SPACE. THIS DECORATIVE TECHNIQUE ALSO PROMOTES SAFETY BY MAKING THE DARK WOODEN TREADS AND HANDRAIL MORE PROMINENT ON THE SHARPLY TWISTING STAIRCASE. **Opposite:** A POTTED TREE SOARING UP TOWARD THE SECOND STORY IS THE FOCAL POINT OF THIS GARDEN-LOVER'S FOYER. HOWEVER, A MAHOGANY SECRETARY OFF TO THE SIDE HOLDS ITS OWN AS A POWERFUL FORCE IN THE ENTRY, THANKS TO ITS MAJESTIC STATURE. THIS REGAL PIECE ALSO SUPPLIES USEFUL STORAGE SPACE FOR BOOKS, CORRESPONDENCE, AND VARIOUS ODDS AND ENDS.

date aria, date luce

GRAND ENTRANCES

There is nothing like the sensation of making a grand entrance. What better way to give guests this privilege than by presenting them with a spacious foyer?

Whether the decor is lavish or understated, a large foyer exudes a feeling of luxury thanks to its size. With its grand character, it can make everything from a casual visit to a black-tie gathering seem like a gala affair, but special care must be taken to ensure that such an entry does not seem overly imposing. The most successful foyers achieve a delicate balance between formality and hospitality, encouraging guests to revel in the splendor of the setting.

Since they are free from space constraints, grand foyers can include large pieces of furniture such as sofas, center tables, or even chaise lounges in place of the chairs and console tables usually found in smaller entries. But despite the seemingly limitless amount of space, large entries often enlist only a few tasteful furnishings, opting instead to display sculpture, artwork, or a jungle's worth of plants. Whether decorated to look like a castle hall, a sophisticated gallery, or simply an elegant prelude to the home, spacious foyers are sure to infuse those who enter with a feeling of importance.

Opposite: THIS PALATIAL FOYER MAKES WONDERFUL USE OF ITS HIGH, ARCHED CEILING. A RICHLY HUED PAINTING OF A CASTLE AND GROUNDS IMMEDIATELY DRAWS THE EYE UP, AND ITS SEMICIRCULAR SHAPE EMPHASIZES THE GRACEFUL CURVE OF THE CEILING. SIMPLE WHITE COLUMNS FOCUS ATTENTION ON THE HEIGHT OF THE ROOM AND THE DETAILED ARTWORK ABOVE. **Above:** AS IF BRIDGING TIME, THIS ENTRY COMBINES TOUCHES OF THE PAST WITH POSTMODERN ARCHITECTURE. BAROQUE PEDESTALS, REGENCY CHAIRS, AND A CHIPPENDALE MIRROR RECALL THE REFINEMENT OF DAYS GONE BY. BUT COOL GRAY WALLS, FLOATING STAIRS, AND A SLATE FLOOR EVOKE A SLEEK CONTEMPORARY TONE THAT ANCHORS THE FOYER IN THE PRESENT. A COPPER LANTERNLIKE FIXTURE HANGS OVERHEAD, HEIGHTENING THE METALLIC LOOK CREATED BY THE SPACE'S MANY SILVERY GRAY TOUCHES.

Above, left: A SCINTILLATING ARRAY OF CHANDELIERS DAZZLES THE EYE AND SPARKS CONVERSATION IN THIS TWO-STORY ENTRANCE. AS LIGHT IS EMITTED FROM THE GLITTERING GOLD-TONED FIXTURES, IT PLAYFULLY BOUNCES OFF THE GLASS PANES OF THE AREA'S WINDOWS. WHILE ONE WINDOW OFFERS A BREATHTAKING VIEW OF THE OUTDOORS, THE OTHER IS FITTED INTO AN INTERIOR WALL, ALLOWING THE LUMINESCENT DISPLAY TO BE ENJOYED FROM A SECOND-STORY ROOM. **Above, right:** FANCIFUL GLAZED DOORS WITH ELEGANT TRACERY HELP SET THE LUXURIOUS TONE OF THIS FOYER. ADORNED WITH EMPIRE STYLING, THE SPACE BOASTS LAVISH DRAPERIES AND A PAIR OF GILT SCONCES. THE GLEAMING ANGELIC FIXTURES GRACIOUSLY LIGHT THE WAY FOR VISITORS, AS THOUGH GUIDING ERRANT WANDERERS ALONG A VIRTUOUS PATH. **Opposite:** HIGH CEILINGS, ELABORATE CHANDELIERS, AND RICH ARCHITECTURAL DETAILS GIVE THIS ENTRANCE HALL A HIGHLY DIGNIFIED APPEARANCE. FORMAL WOOD FURNISHINGS—INCLUDING ELEGANT PIER TABLES, SUMPTUOUSLY UPHOLSTERED SOFAS, AND A DISTINGUISHED GRANDFATHER CLOCK—LOOK EXCEPTIONALLY BEAUTIFUL THANKS TO THE SOFT GREEN AND IVORY COLOR SCHEME, WHICH PROVIDES A FLATTERING BACKDROP. WHEN THE HALL IS ILLUMINATED, THE CREAMY PALETTE TAKES ON A SERENE AURA.

Right: Reminiscent of a museum hall, this immense foyer showcases primitive-looking pieces of sculpture. Thanks to a dramatic lighting technique, the shadows of these carved figures playfully dance along the smooth, white backdrop. Recessed lights and polished hardwood floors contribute to the entry's streamlined look, while a neutral palette imbues the space with sophistication.

Opposite: BLESSED WITH A ROTUNDA FOR AN ENTRY, THE OWNERS OF THIS HOME TRANSFORMED THE SPACE INTO A SITTING AREA. WHILE A GOLDEN TEXTURED WALL TREATMENT ENVELOPS THE ROOM IN WARMTH, A DEEP BLUE PAINT JOB SPECKLED WITH SHINY GOLD STARS TRANSFORMS THE DOMED CEILING INTO A NIGHTTIME SKY. AN INVITING OVERSTUFFED COUCH PROVIDES THE PERFECT SPOT FOR STARGAZING. **Left:** VARIOUS DECORATIVE ACCENTS INFUSE THIS FOYER WITH AN AIR OF MAGNIFICENCE. AGAINST A FAUX STONE PAINT TREATMENT, A SHINY GOLD- AND COPPER-TONED MIRROR FRAME PROVIDES A SPLASH OF OPULENCE, AS DOES A STACK OF LEATHER-BOUND BOOKS EMBOSSED WITH GOLD LEAF. ELEGANT CRYSTAL BAUBLES DANGLE LIKE DEW DROPS FROM THE BRANCHING ARMS OF A PAIR OF SCONCES, PROVIDING A SPARKLING TOUCH WHEN THEY CAPTURE THE LIGHT.

Opposite: A PREDOMINANTLY BLUE MURAL WITH PINKISH CLOUDS LENDS THIS FOYER AN ETHEREAL QUALITY. A FANLIGHT AND SIDELIGHTS CONTRIBUTE TO THE AIRY

FEELING, WHILE A STEEPLY ASCENDING STAIRCASE SEEMS TO REACH UP TO THE HEAVENS. BACK ON TERRA FIRMA, AN ORIENTAL RUG SOFTENS WOODEN FLOORBOARDS,

WHILE ITS ROUND CENTRAL DESIGN MIRRORS THE MEDALLION DIRECTLY OVERHEAD. **Above:** BRANCHES OF LEAVES ON A WALLPAPER PRINT MINGLE WITH THE REAL THING

TO CREATE A JUNGLE PARADISE IN THIS EDENIC FOYER. A GARDEN BENCH ENHANCES THE OUTDOOR FEELING, AS DOES A SMALL RABBIT SCULPTURE RESTING QUIETLY UNDER

THE SHELTER OF LUSH FOLIAGE. OVERHEAD, A RECESSED CEILING ILLUMINATED WITH COVE LIGHTS CREATES THE IMAGE OF A GLOWING SUN.

Above: A SERIES OF THREE ARCHES, ANGLED SO AS TO FORM AN OCTAGON WITH THE FOYER'S WALLS, SETS THE AREA OFF FROM THE REST OF THE HOME. ECHOING THE SHAPE OF THE DOOR FRAME, THESE ARCHES PROVIDE GRAND PASSAGES TO THE SPACE BEYOND. A VIVIDLY PATTERNED AREA RUG MIRRORS THE SHAPE OF THE FOYER, WHICH IS ALSO EMPHASIZED BY THE DIRECTION OF THE FLOORBOARDS. **Right:** THE ABUNDANCE OF STONE IN THIS FOYER IMPARTS THE DRAMA OF AN ANCIENT CASTLE. WHILE A WARMING TAPESTRY RUG COVERS A GOOD PORTION OF THE FLOOR, THE POINTS OF AN UNDERLYING STARBURST DESIGN REMAIN VISIBLE. A LAVISH SWEEPING STAIRCASE ADDS TO THE GRANDEUR, RUNNING AROUND THE ROOM'S CIRCUMFERENCE LIKE A DRAGON CHASING ITS TAIL.

Sources

ARCHITECTS AND INTERIOR DESIGNERS

(page 2)
Wendy Bolland, designer
Manchester, MA
(978) 526-4392

(page 17 bottom)
Perry Dean Rogers and
Partners, architects
Boston, MA
(617) 423-0100

(page 19)
Bullock & Company, builders
Creekmore, Ontario
(705) 466-2505

(page 20)
Patricia Borba McDonald,
designer
San Jose, CA
(408) 292-6997

(page 24 left)
Winton Scott, architect
Portland, ME
(207) 774-4811

(pages 26, 27)
John Silverio, architect
Lincolnville, ME
(207) 763-3885

(pages 28, 38)
Deborah T. Lipner, Ltd.,
designer
Greenwich, CT
(203) 629-2626

(pages 30–31)
Celeste Cooper of The Cooper
Group, designer
Boston, MA
(617) 266-2288

(page 34)
Susan Hollis, designer
Concord, MA
(978) 371-2622

(page 35 left)
Allison Holland, designer
Honolulu, HI
(808) 955-1465

(page 44)
C + J Katz Studio, designers
Boston, MA
(617) 367-0537

(page 45)
Centerbrook Architects
Essex, CT
(860) 767-0175

(page 48 left)
Tom O'Toole, designer
New York, NY
(212) 348-0639

(page 49 right)
Van Martin Rowe, designer
Pasadena, CA
(818) 577-4736

(page 51 left)
Thomas M. Beeton Inc.,
designers
Beverly Hills, CA
(310) 247-0325

(pages 54, 59, 60 left)
Brian Murphy, designer
Santa Monica, CA
(310) 459-0955

(page 55)
Samuel Botero Associates,
designers
New York, NY
(212) 935-5155

(page 58)
Paula McChesney, designer
San Mateo, CA
(415) 343-9610

(page 62)
Design Alliance, architects
Portland, ME
(207) 773-1756

(page 67)
Parish-Hadley Associates, Inc.,
designers
New York, NY
(212) 888-7979

(page 68)
Chris Kellogg, architect
Portland, ME
(207) 775-2226

PHOTOGRAPHY CREDITS

PHOTOGRAPHY CREDITS

©Chris Drake/The Interior Archive: 40 (designer: Graham Carr)

©Phillip H. Ennis: 21, 44 left (designer: Design Logic), 55 (designer: Samuel Botero Associates), 60 right (designer: Andrew Tedesco), 67 (designer: Parish-Hadley)

©Tria Giovan: 24 right, 43

©Nancy Hill: 28 (designer: Deborah T. Lipner, Ltd.; Floor: Viva Crozier), 38 (designer: Deborah T. Lipner, Ltd.), 57 (designer: David Parker)

©image/dennis krukowski: 17 top (designer: Burgess Lea), 32 (designer: Jean P. Simmers Ltd. Interiors), 39 (designer: David Laurance), 48 left (designer: Tom O'Toole)

©David Livingston: 20 (designer: Patricia Borba McDonald), 35 right (designer: Candace Barnes), 35 left (designer: Allison Holland), 58 (designer: Paula McChesney)

©Richard Mandelkorn: 12 (architect: Lindsay Associates, Inc.), 17 bottom (architect: Perry Dean Rogers Partners), 30–31 (designer: Celeste Cooper of The Cooper Group), 36 right

©Keith Scott Morton: 13 bottom, 23 right, 50

©David Phelps: 11, 13 top, 52 (courtesy *American Homestyle & Gardening* magazine), 18 (courtesy *First For Woman* magazine)

©Paul Rocheleau: 22 (architect: Edward Goodell), 36 left, 61, 66

©Eric Roth: 2 (designer: Wendy Bolland), 34 (designer: Susan Hollis), 44 right (designer: C+J Katz Studio), 46

©Tim Street-Porter: 6 (designer: Jarrett Hedborg), 10 (architect: Frank Israel), 14 left (designer: Neil Korpinen), 14 right (designer: Kathryn Ireland), 16 (designer: Hutton Wilkinson), 23 left (designer: Roy McMakin), 30 left (designer: Brian Murphy), 41 (architect: Piers Gough), 47 (designer: Barbara Barry), 51 right (designer: Paulene Morton), 53 (designer: Holly Leuders), 68–69 (architect: Cliff May)

©Brian Vanden Brink: 8, 15, 19 (builder: Bullock & Company), 24 left (architect: Winton Scott), 25, 26-27 (architect: John Silverio), 27 right (John Silverio), 29, 42, 45 (architect: Centerbrook Architects), 48 right, 56, 62–63 (architect: Design Alliance), 68 left (architect: Chris Kellogg)

©Dominique Vorillon: 33 (designer: Arroyo), 37, 49 left (designer: Deborah Jones), 49 right (designer: Van Martin Rowe), 51 left (designer: Tom Beeton), 54, 59, 60 left (designer: Brian Murphy), 64 (designer: Michael Anderson), 65 (designer: Laurie Steichen)

INDEX

Arches, 68
Architectural details, 10–27
Arts and Crafts theme, 20
Artwork, 43

Back entrance, 48
Balustrade(s), 12
  grid-patterned, 24
  log, 19
Bannister, 51
Beach theme, 49
Bookcase, 8
Bullseye windows, 26–27

Carpeting, 8
Ceilings
  arched, 58
  recessed, 67
Chair rails, 12
Chandeliers, 49, 60–61
Checkerboard painted floors,
  17, 20, 31, 36, 39, 42, 44
Closet(s), 9
  creating, 53
  doors, paintings on, 29
Coat racks, 9
Collections, 22, 43, 45, 49,
  51, 62–63
Color, effect of, 29, 30, 34–35
Columns, 21, 23, 58
Console table, 9, 20, 43
Corner shelf, 54
Cornice, 12, 31
Country theme, 49

Dadoes, 12, 31
Display niches, 43
Door(s)
  architectural styles of, 11
  double, 11, 16
  French, 12, 37
  glazed, 60

massive, 10
  Spanish Colonial Revival, 14
Doorways, 13, 20
Double-door entrance, 11, 16

Empire styling, 60
Entryway, creating of, 45

Fanlight, 12, 66
Faux finishes
  marble, 29, 32
  stone, 29, 65
Flooring/floors
  choice of, 7
  hardwood, 7, 62–63
  marble, 7, 20
  painted, 10, 36, 55
  slate, 29, 59
  stenciled, 28
  stone, 7, 69
  terra-cotta, 16, 48, 52
  tile, 21
Floral arrangements, 50
French doors, 12, 37
Furniture, 7
  in grand entrances, 59

Glass arrangements, 24
Glass panels, in door, 12,
  14–15, 23, 26–27
Grand entrances, 58–69
Greenery, 48, 57

Hardwood floors, 7, 62–63

Leaded glass, 13
Lighting
  cove, 44
  recessed, 31
  and safety, 9
  use of, 8–9
Louvered panels, 39

Marble floors, 7
  checkerboard, 20
Mirrors, 9, 42, 48, 65
  full-length, 43
Mural, 66

Oriental rugs, 17, 66

Paint, power of, 28–41
Painted floors, 55
Paintings, on closet doors, 29
Paint treatments, 7
Paneling, 12, 13
Pedestal table, 50
Picture rails, 34
Pier tables, 61
Pilaster, 35
Postmodern architecture, 59

Reading nook, 47
Recessed lighting, 31
Rotunda, 64
Runners, 25, 31
  painted, 32, 36
  using staining techniques, 38
Rustic entryway, 19

Safety
  lighting and, 9
  painted stairs and, 56
Sconces, 9, 42, 48, 60, 65
Seating area(s), 9, 46, 64
Secretary, 57
Shelves, 43, 54
Sidelights, 8, 18, 37, 39, 66
  glass-block, 10
Side table, 43, 49
Slate floor, 29, 59
Small entryways, 42–57
Southwestern theme, 16, 52
Spanish Colonial Revival door,
14

Spiral staircase, 15
Spotlights, 9
Stained glass windows, 23
Staining techniques, 38
Staircases, 12, 56, 66, 69
  branched, 25
  floating, 59
  spiral, 15
  steep, 41
  swirling, 47
  terra-cotta, 10
Stencils, 32
  for borders, 29
  for floor, 28
Still life, 7
Stone floor, 7, 69
Storage space, 9

Table(s)
  console, 9, 20, 43
  pedestal, 50
  pier, 61
  side, 43, 49
Tile floors, 21
  handpainted, 10
  terra-cotta, 16, 48, 52
Transoms, 8, 17
Trompe l'oeil, 29, 36, 39–40

Umbrella stand, 9, 43, 45

Vinyl, 8

Wallpaper, 42, 55–56, 67
Walls
  adobe, 16
  curving, 14
Windows, 60
  bullseye, 26–27
  stained glass, 23